The Science of Senses

How Animals SEE

Cavendish Square
New York

Joanne Mattern

Published in 2019 by Cavendish Square Publishing, LLC
243 5th Avenue, Suite 136, New York, NY 10016

Copyright © 2019 by Cavendish Square Publishing, LLC

First Edition

No part of this publication may be reproduced, stored in a retrieval system, or transmitted in any form or by any means—electronic, mechanical, photocopying, recording, or otherwise—without the prior permission of the copyright owner. Request for permission should be addressed to Permissions, Cavendish Square Publishing, 243 5th Avenue, Suite 136, New York, NY 10016. Tel (877) 980-4450; fax (877) 980-4454.

Website: cavendishsq.com

This publication represents the opinions and views of the author based on his or her personal experience, knowledge, and research. The information in this book serves as a general guide only. The author and publisher have used their best efforts in preparing this book and disclaim liability rising directly or indirectly from the use and application of this book.

All websites were available and accurate when this book was sent to press.

Library of Congress Cataloging-in-Publication Data

Names: Mattern, Joanne, 1963- author.
Title: How animals see / Joanne Mattern.
Description: First edition. | New York : Cavendish Square, 2019. | Series: The science of senses | Audience: Grades 2-5. | Includes index. Identifiers: LCCN 2018023392 (print) | LCCN 2018025453 (ebook) | ISBN 9781502642073 (ebook) | ISBN 9781502642066 (library bound) | ISBN 9781502642042 (paperback) | ISBN 9781502642059 (6 pack)
Subjects: LCSH: Vision--Juvenile literature. | Eye--Juvenile literature. | Senses and sensation--Juvenile literature. | Animals--Juvenile literature.
Classification: LCC QP475.7 (ebook) | LCC QP475.7 .M38 2019 (print) | DDC 573.8/8--dc23
LC record available at https://lccn.loc.gov/2018023392

Editorial Director: David McNamara
Editor: Kristen Susienka
Copy Editor: Nathan Heidelberger
Associate Art Director: Alan Sliwinski
Designer: Ginny Kemmerer
Production Coordinator: Karol Szymczuk
Photo Research: J8 Media

The photographs in this book are used by permission and through the courtesy of: Cover DenisaPro/Shutterstock.com; p. 4 Flip de Nooyer/Minden Pictures/Getty Images; p. 6 Joe Hendrickson/Shutterstock.com; p. 7 Elana Erasmus/Shutterstock.com; p. 8 CreativeNature_nl/iStock; p. 9 HelloRF Zcool/Shutterstock.com; p. 10 (top) Sergey Uryadnikov/Shutterstock.com; p. 10 (bottom) Joel Sartore/National Geographic/Getty Images; p. 11 (top) Jakub Kaliszewski/Moment/Getty Images; p. 11 (bottom) Dan Kitwood/Getty Images; p. 12 Aedka Studio/Shutterstock.com; p. 14 Sari ONeal/Shutterstock.com; p. 15 Ron Erwin/All Canada Photos/Getty Images; p. 17 Dorling Kindersley/Getty Images; p. 19 Dirk Ercken/Shutterstock.com; p. 20 Peopleimages/E+/Getty Images; p. 22 PeopleImages/iStock; p. 23 Dmitry A/Shutterstock.com; p. 25 Lotus_studio/Shutterstock.com; p. 26 m-imagephotography/iStock; p. 27 Cordelia Molloy/Science Source.

Printed in the United States of America

CONTENTS

One   The Sense of Sight 5

Two   How Seeing Works 13

Three   Seeing the World 21

Glossary 28

Find Out More 29

Index 31

About the Author 32

This cat's eyes help it find and sneak up on a crow.

Chapter One

The Sense of Sight

The sense of sight is very important for almost every animal on Earth. Seeing tells animals what is happening in the world around them. If danger is nearby, an animal can see it coming in time to get away. If the animal is hungry, its eyes help it look for food to eat.

Different Eyes

Not every animal's eyes are the same. Each animal's eyes have **adapted** to where it lives and how it lives. Animals that are **prey** need to see so they can spot a **predator** before it attacks and eats them.

A deer's eyes are on the sides of its head to help it see predators coming too close.

Animals like rabbits and deer have eyes on the sides of their heads. The position of their eyes means that the animals can see a wide area without turning their heads. This makes it easier to spot a predator coming close.

Predators, on the other hand, usually have eyes that face forward. This helps animals like cheetahs or wolves follow their prey. Owls have large eyes compared to their body size. This helps them see their prey, even in the dark.

Light and Dark

Other animal eyes are adapted to the places where they live. Animals that live in the dark often have large eyes with large **pupils**. Having large pupils allows animals to gather more light. Taking in light lets animals see.

Other animals have very small eyes because the sense of sight is not as important to them. One example

This cheetah keeps its eyes on its prey as it chases the animal.

> **FACT!**
>
> Most animals have two eyes. Some sea creatures, like a scallop, have more than one hundred eyes!

is a shrew. A shrew lives underground. It doesn't need good eyesight in the dark under the dirt. Instead, it uses its sense of smell to find food.

Special Eyes

Animals that live in water often have special eyes to help them see. Some fish and mammals have eyes that have adapted to seeing underwater. Water affects how animals see light. Also, some water is dirty and hard to see through.

A shrew doesn't need to see well, so its eyes are very tiny.

Insects often have **compound** eyes, or eyes with many **lenses**. Each lens sees an image. Having many lenses helps insects see movements much better than people. It also helps insects avoid danger.

The many lenses in a fly's eyes help it see movement and avoid danger.

No matter what an animal's eyes look like, they are an important part of a creature's everyday life. An animal that cannot see has a hard time surviving in the wild. Eyes work in many important ways.

FACT!

The giant squid has the largest eyes on the planet. Each eye is almost 10 inches (25.4 centimeters) wide. Big eyes help the squid see well in the dark waters where it lives.

ANIMALS AROUND THE WORLD

NORTH AMERICA: An eagle flies high in the sky, looking for prey far below with its excellent sense of sight.

SOUTH AMERICA: The four-eyed fish likes to stay close to the water's surface. It has eyes on top of its head. Each eye is divided in two parts. The top part of its eyes can see above the water. The bottom part can see below the water.

10 How Animals See

EUROPE: A deer has eyes on the sides of its head. This helps it see predators in areas next to them.

ASIA: The dragonfly has the largest eyes of any insect. It can also see more colors than people can. These special eyes help the dragonfly find food.

The Sense of Sight

This close-up photo of a gecko's eye shows its iris and pupil.

Chapter Two

How Seeing Works

Eyes have many parts. For most animals, the parts are the same: an iris, a pupil, rods, and cones. The parts work together to help animals and people see.

Finding Light

The iris is the colorful part of an eye. It is a muscle that surrounds the dark spot in an eye. The spot is called a pupil. Light enters the

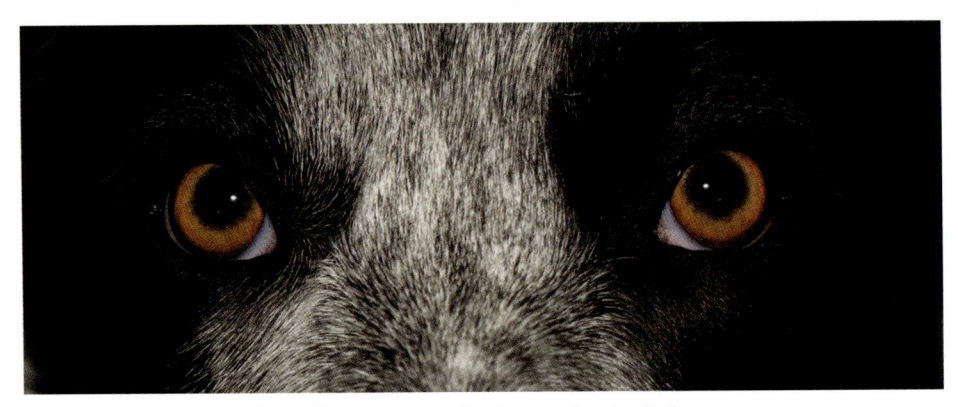

This dog's pupils are big. They need to be big to let in light.

eye through the pupil. The iris controls how much light enters the eye. When there is a lot of light, like on a sunny day, the iris makes the pupil smaller. When there is not a lot of light, the iris makes the pupil bigger.

The more light that enters the eye, the better the animal sees. Animals with large pupils can usually see better than animals with small pupils. This is true at night, when it is dark. Large pupils allow more light into the eye and help the animal see. That is why most **nocturnal** animals have large pupils.

NIGHT EYES

Some nocturnal animals have such large pupils that there is no room in their eyes for muscles to move the eyes back and forth or up and down. Animals like the owl have eyes that only face forward. To make up for this problem, these animals have necks that are easy to move and twist. An owl can turn its head almost completely around. Instead of moving its eyes, the animal moves its whole head to see what is around it.

An owl stares straight at the camera. These birds can't move their eyes, but they can turn their heads almost completely around.

How Seeing Works

> **FACT!**
> Penguins have special eyes that let them see clearly underwater.

Once light enters the eye, it hits a lens. The lens **focuses** the light. It sends a picture to a part of the back of the eye. This part is called the **retina**. The retina is connected to an **optic nerve**. An optic nerve sends the picture to the brain. The brain reads the picture and identifies what it is.

Rods and Cones

Seeing is more than just light. It also includes color. At the back of the eye are special cells. Some of these cells are called rods. Rods see black, white, and gray. They can also see the shape of an object. Rods gather light to see in the dark. However, they cannot see color.

Other cells are called cones. Cones see color. They sense the colors in the waves of light entering the eye and send messages to the brain. There are three different kinds of cones. One kind sees red. The second kind sees green. The third kind sees blue. The eye can combine these three colors into millions of other colors. The more cones an animal's eye has, the more colors it can see.

Not all animals have the same number of rods and cones. For example, dogs have fewer cones than

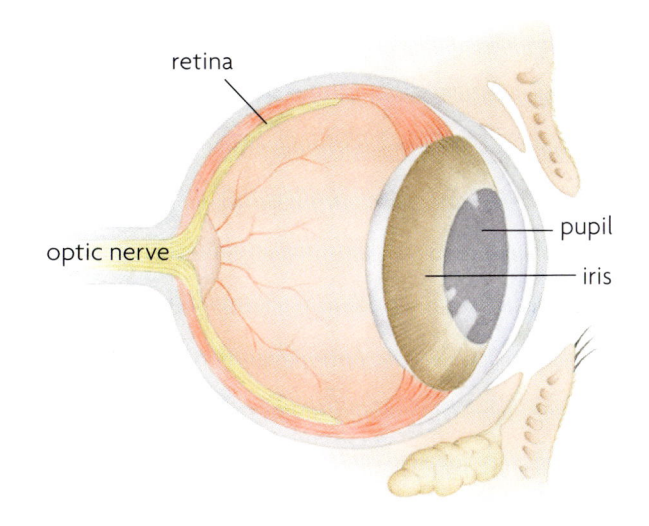

This diagram of a dog's eye shows its pupil and iris. Behind them are the retina and optic nerve that help the animal see.

How Seeing Works 17

> **FACT!**
> A chameleon can move each eye by itself.

people. That means they see fewer colors than we do. Geckos, which are active at night, have more rods than animals that are active during the day. An animal's eyes adapt to the place where it lives. This is true whether the animal lives in a bright sunny desert or a dark cave.

Seeing color can be very important to an animal. Many animals are attracted to bright colors. They know these colors are clues to finding food. Hummingbirds and butterflies go to flowers that are brightly colored. They know these flowers have food that is good to eat.

Other animals use color as a warning. If an animal is poisonous, like the colorful poison dart frog, a predator

When predators see the poison dart frog's bright colors, they know to stay away.

that sees it knows to stay away. The bright color sends a message that says, "Danger! Do not eat me!"

Muscle Movement

Most animals can move their eyes around. Muscles in each eye move the eye up and down, or back and forth. This helps the animal see all around it. For example, an animal such as a jaguar can look in every direction to spot its prey.

People use their eyes to find and choose food, just like animals do.

Chapter Three

Seeing the World

Humans see in much the same way that animals see. Like many animals, humans have eyes with an iris and a pupil. These let light into the eye. If the light is too bright, we cannot see well. It might even hurt. When there is too much light, the iris makes the pupil smaller.

Like an animal's eyes, a human's iris makes the pupil bigger when there is not a lot of light. This lets more light into the eye. Now we can see better.

Just like animal eyes, human eyes have a lens to focus the light onto a retina. Human retinas also have rods and cones. Rods and cones let us see light and colors.

A human eye has the same parts as an animal's eye.

Information Everywhere

Both humans and animals use their eyes to see the world. An animal looks around to see what the weather is like. It sees where it lives. It sees what is happening around it.

When you're hungry, you can open the refrigerator and use your eyes to see food you can eat. When an animal is hungry, it looks around. Its eyes tell it if there is something good to eat. It can see exactly where to go to get its next meal.

Your eyes can warn you of danger. If you see a car coming or a dangerous spot on the sidewalk, you know to stop or take a different path. If an animal sees a predator coming, it knows to run to safety. Just like a stop sign or a red light tells cars to stop, colors can tell animals to stay away and stay safe.

FACT!

A pigeon's eyes are on the sides of its head. It can see in almost every direction—even behind!

Finding Our Way

Humans use sight to move around rooms or outside. Animals also use their eyes to get around safely. A fish can see rocks, ships, or other objects in its way. Looking around lets the fish swim safely around these objects. The same is true of animals on land.

Our eyes are made to help us see things that are important to us. Animal eyes are specially made too. Insects have compound eyes to help them sense danger in time to get away. Owls have huge eyes that help them find prey on the ground. Animals that are active in the dark have larger eyes and larger pupils. These large pupils gather in as much light as possible. This makes getting around in the dark easier and safer.

A fish's eyes are specially made to help them see underwater.

FACT!

A bird called a buzzard can see small rodents from 15,000 feet (4,572 meters) in the air.

Just like people, most animals get a lot of their information from their eyes. Sight is an amazing sense. It helps animals stay alive, no matter where they live.

Our eyes help us see wonderful things as we look around our world.

EYES THAT SHINE

A cat's eyes reflect light. This makes them appear to glow in the dark.

Have you ever seen a cat's eyes glow in the dark? A cat has a special part in its eye. This part is called the tapetum. It helps cats see in the dark. The tapetum reflects light. This makes the animal's eyes appear to glow at night.

Seeing the World

GLOSSARY

adapted Adjusted to new conditions.

compound Made of many parts.

focuses Makes an image clearer.

lenses Parts of the eye that focus light.

nocturnal Active at night.

optic nerve The area at the back of the eye that carries images from the eye to the brain.

predator An animal that hunts other animals for food.

prey Animals that are eaten for food.

pupils Dark spots in the eyes that let in light.

retina A part at the back of the eye that receives light. It contains rods and cones.

Find Out More

Books

Holland, Mary. *Animal Eyes*. Mount Pleasant, SC: Arbordale Publishing, 2014.

Honders, Christine. *How Cats and Other Animals See at Night*. New York: PowerKids Press, 2016.

Websites

How Do Animals See in the Dark?

http://mocomi.com/how-do-animals-see-in-the-dark

This site describes the special features that allow animals to see in the dark.

How Do Other Animals See the World?

http://www.nhm.ac.uk/discover/how-do-other-animals-see-the-world.html

Learn facts about different animal eyes here.

FIND OUT MORE CONTINUED

The World Through Animal Eyes

https://www.kidsdiscover.com/teacherresources/the-world-through-animal-eyes

Animals see the world differently than people do! This website explains how and why.

Videos

How Animals and People See the World Differently

https://www.youtube.com/watch?v=6HWVgQdSTDQ

This video looks at many different animal eyes and compares them to the eyes of people.

How Animals See the World

https://www.youtube.com/watch?v=6hYaT4gvjNc

Watch this video for an up-close look at how different animals see the world.

Page numbers in **boldface** are illustrations. Entries in **boldface** are glossary terms.

adapted, 6–8, 18
brain, 16–17
color, 11, 16–19, 22–23
compound, 9, 24
cones, 13, 17–18, 22
dark, 7–9, 14, 17–18, 25, 27
fish, 8, 10, **10**, 24, **25**
focuses, 16, 22
insects, 9, **9**, 11, **11**, 24

irises, **12**, 13–14, **17**, 21–22, **22**
lenses, 9, 16, 22
muscles, 13, 15, 19
nocturnal, 14–15
optic nerve, 16, **17**
owls, 6–7, 15, **15**, 24
predator, 6, 11, 18–19, 23
prey, 6–7, 10, 19, 24
pupils, 7, **12**, 13–15, **14**, **17**, 21–22, **22**, 25
retina, 16, **17**, 22
rods, 13, 16–18, 22

Index 31

Joanne Mattern is the author of hundreds of nonfiction books for children and young adults. Animals are her favorite subjects to write about, along with sports, history, and biography. Mattern lives in New York State with her husband, children, and an assortment of pets.